ENGLISH
FOR
AMERICANS

with a
sense of humour ...

or

All you ever wanted to know
about the English Language
but were afraid to ask.

by **M. TRACEY**

COPYRIGHT © M. TRACEY 1984

ISBN No. 0–9510223–0–X

PUBLISHED BY MANIPURI PRESS (LONDON) 1985

PRINTED BY SUNCROSS PRESS LTD · ISLEWORTH · MIDDX

About the Author

Maureen Tracey (known as Tracey)—Born in Huddersfield, West Yorkshire. Educated there and in Leeds. Started work in the office of Standard Fireworks and learned very early on that office life was too static for me. Therefore decided to try all types of work and have done almost every possible job since then. As my brother said "She only has to work down the Pit (mine) and she has done everything".

But mainly—spent many years in the theatre as stage manager, later character actress in Rep., T.V. and one film!! Finally got tired of not eating and went into Travel. As a Tour Manager I have travelled many places in the world. I now work for an American Company—but my home is in London—Give travel talks, with a difference, and wondering if I should change my career yet again???

Love of music, travel, excitement, adventure, people, elegance, beautiful things, art, conversation, wine, solitude . . . I gave up the idea of marriage, when I discovered the boy I was to marry did not like violins.

About the Artist

Molly Blake was born in St. Albans, Hertfordshire. But has lived most of her life in London.

Educated (after a fashion) in Suffolk and at the Central School of Art, her first job was in Advertising.

Neice of actor Sir John Mills and daughter of Annette Mills, much loved personality in the early days of Childrens Television, Molly presented her own glove puppet programme, "Prudence Kitten" for some years for the B.B.C.

Having raised a family, she now works at the Headquarters of a Charity organisation where her drawings help to enliven the staff magazine. Hopes one day to become a "serious" painter. (Clown playing Hamlet?)

To

DONALD
(my favourite brother)

Acknowledgements

My thanks to:–Jan Stussy, Artist and Lecturer in Art, Los Angeles, who pushed me more than anyone to write this book and to Judge Al Margolis, also of L.A., who made sure I knew all the ins and outs of Publishing—by sending me a very helpful book *"How to get happily published"*. A special thank-you to Molly Blake for drawing my thoughts so well and for the help she has given me—with this—my first book.

Foreword

If you are an American visitor here or English-speaking going to the U.S.A., then here is a bit of painless knowledge to help you on your way. A bit of lighthearted reading to put you straight on the differences between English-English and American-English. After all, how many English people abroad would dream of asking for the bathroom in a restaurant??? And what problems for the American who happens to say, "I will wash-up while you are fixing my order". Now any waiter worth his salt would politely ask regarding means of payment I am sure, did he not know the American meaning for this.

So many different ways of saying the same thing, can cause embarrassment at the time, but make us laugh later.

This is not going to get the Nobel Prize for literature—no—it is just a fun thing . . . so enjoy the anecdotes with me about some of my embarrassing moments while escorting American tourists, and make sure, at the same time, you do not fall into the same trap.

"Why don't you write a book?

How many of my friends have said that. Finally, while escorting a group of Americans around Africa, I made my mind up to put pen to paper. What caused me to do this was the difference between words and meanings of our common language. I must say during my time in the travel business we've had a lot of laughs over the different meanings. One of the many things I like about the Americans is their love of a good laugh. They have the capacity to enjoy life. Of course, I can give examples, and I'm sure you can, of very dreary Americans. But I speak generally: I speak of the majority. Make them laugh, and you've a friend for life. Mind you, I believe if you can make anyone laugh, American or otherwise, half the battle is over. The friendship has started.

I must say at times the laugh has been on me, but then the funniest stories are usually against oneself, aren't they? In fact, the first time I realised there was a difference between our language, the joke was on me. Anyway, why should I tell you my best story first? The rest of the book would be an anti-climax, and unless you read this, how can I hope you'll buy my next one? And I need the money—or my landlord does.

Of course, you have to remember I've met people from all over the States, and words do alter in meaning even from one state to another, and although some of your meanings and ours can be understood even though the words differ, it's fun to compare and have a laugh doing so.

1

On arrival at London Airport, the porter who carries your bags may ask if he should also take your carrier-bag. Do not be surprised, he means your tote bag. When he asks you to join the queue for a taxi, he means you will have to stand in line.

Once you are in the taxi, you will go into London, or 'down town', as you will say, along what we call the motorway and you call the freeway. This, to you, may be a divided highway but, to us, it is a dual carriageway.

When you come to the overpass—guess what? It is a flyover.

On arrival at your hotel your bags will be unloaded from the taxi platform next to the driver's seat. The London taxi does have a small trunk but seldom used; in fact, we say boot of a car, not trunk of a car.

If you want to get really confused, try this: A trunk, to us, would mean a large not-wanted-on-voyage type piece of baggage. A boot can also be a lace-up type of footwear for men or the type of footwear worn by women in cold weather, can also be a slang term for being dismissed from one's work—"To get the boot". How it even came into the word to mean trunk of a car I do not know. The word trunk came into being due to the fact that the first cars did actually have a trunk attached to the back of the car for example the first Rolls Royce. A trunk got its name due to the fact the earliest ones—were indeed a hollowed-out piece of tree trunk. So you see, we even have more than one meaning for our own words, and still do not understand why we call things what we do. While we are at it, change bonnet and hood around too.

In the lobby, which we usually call foyer, (this also applies to a theatre or cinema—sorry, movie-house as well) you will be checked in by the receptionist, whom I know you call desk clerk (and to confuse the issue we pronounce it clark) but we like the word receptionist. sounds more welcoming.

Then the confusion of which floor you are on. What we call the ground floor, you call the first floor, making our first floor your second, so bear this in mind when pressing the button in the lift (elevator), or you will finish up on the wrong floor.

Do not ask for a cot.

If you need an extra bed in your room, do not ask for a cot. To us a cot is one of those railed-in beds for children which most Americans call a crib. A crib, to us, is for a newborn or very young baby—sort of all frilly and small—the cot, not the baby. So be sure to say, "We would like an extra bed".

When you want to make a reservation at the theatre, we say, "We would like to book a seat". At a restaurant, we "book a table".

4

Maybe you are going to stay with a family. Uh-u...
More language difficulties! Let us suppose you go by
railroad. You will not be going on a locomotive, but a
train, and remember to ask for the railway station, not
the railroad station. Incidentally, our trains run on
railway lines, not on a track, and a freight train is called a
goods train and they pull trucks, sometimes they may
be called containers, but only when they are carrying
specialised things like oil, grain etc. I know a truck is
something different to you, but we know that as a lorry,
and the man who drives it is a lorry driver, not a trucker.

The mention of grain reminds me of another
confusing thing. What you would call a field of grain, we
call a corn field. Not exactly correct I know, but that is
what we call it. You see we do not grow corn over here,
well not generally, as it needs more heat than we are
used to. We import it. I remember when I was very
young I used to go to buy this from the shop (store) for
my aunty Nell who kept hens and cocks (roosters) and
chickens. One had to ask for Indian corn—I am not sure
what they feed the hens on now, I guess something less
expensive I am not sure. But in this day and age we
import the corn on the cob, that is what we call the
whole thing, which we cook in salt water and eat with
lashings of butter, then the single grains we buy frozen
or tinned (canned) and call that sweet corn, then again
they grind the dried corn and call it maize, sort of like
your grits or the African meali-meal. This is not used
much, people like me who are adventurous cooks use
it, otherwise it is usually people with an Italian

background, for it is their polenta. No, when we say a corn field, then someone may ask, "What sort of corn", to which we will reply—either barley, wheat, oats, rye, etc. but we just lump it all together under the name corn. So when you read in a novel about . . . "a field of waving corn". . . we are not talking about your corn, but more—a field of wheat, or barley. After all, if some young thing was "running through a field of corn", this would sound romantic to us. To you she would just not be seen at all—as the corn would be higher than her, so the point would be lost; and so would she.

Now you need a ticket. Instead of a one-way ticket we ask for a single ticket. It is nothing to do with your marital status nor with how many people are travelling. Strange, I know, but you can have three or four single tickets, if you wish. If you want a round-trip ticket, then it is a return ticket you will need to buy.

The time-table of train departures you call a schedule. Even here there is a problem, because we say schedule and you say skedule. We use the word for a more informal time-table or programme—for instance, your holiday schedule. We talk about a scheduled flight as opposed to a charter flight, but the flight times are listed on a time-table. Clear?

While we are talking about transport, although we do not have trams any more, they would be what you would call a street-car. Anyone talking about the Underground, or the Tube, means a subway. The only thing we call subway is the one you walk through to cross the road or the track, as you say

A limited stop bus is our version of your rapid transport. Anyway, my bet is you will hire a car and drive yourself. So here are a few more comparisons.

When you fill up, you do it with petrol not gas. Gas, I know, is short for gasolene, but to us, gas means one thing, and that is the sort you use for the gas-cooker or the gas-heater, etc. You buy the gas from what we used to always call a garage, but these days it passes as a petrol station, or what we both sometimes say, a filling station. You would also go to the same place if you had a blow-out; to us, that indicates a really good six- or seven-course meal and nothing to do with tyres at all. So, to be on the safe side, we just say "a burst tyre", or perhaps "a flat tyre", even a "flat". On the other hand, a flat, to us is an apartment to you, just to add to your confusion . . . so your apartment block to us would be simply—a block of flats. 'Condo' or condominium is not known here in this context. We only differentiate between purpose built flats and a conversion. The latter being—say an old Victorian house converted into separate flats (apartments) and would be the nearest we come to your 'condo'. An apartment implies to us— a type of holiday let (rent)—a divided room with simple cooking facilities. A duplex we would know as a semi-detached. We also have a caretaker—in some very expensive blocks. He would be your janitor or super.

"Is this the body shop?

Another difference which I adore is you taking the car along to the body shop. If you asked someone in England where you would find a body shop, now they would either think that you were looking for a Health Club, or maybe a Beauty Parlour. Quite possibly they would think, if a male asked the question, that he was looking for a rather strange massage parlour, which the West End of London has acquired these last few years. Anyway, for sure they would never guess you were only looking for a Panel Beater.

Other items of interest. Muffler is a silencer, antenna an aerial, monkey wrench a spanner, parking lot a car park, and if you feel sleepy or wish to discontinue driving for a while, it is a lay-by where you will park, not a rest stop.

Talking of rest stops. I thought we had enough different ways of saying W.C. But when I first met Americans it came as a surprise to me that W.C. or lavatory were never mentioned; they were disguised as bathroom, (the favourite term), or comfort station, rest room, John, toilet, little girls room, powder room. On one tour, when a lady asked me for the latter, a man's voice from the back of the coach said, "For God's sake do not strike a match in there!" So, when you arrive at your friends, if you ask for the bathroom they may think all you want to do is wash your hands and send you to the bathroom literally.

In some homes the bathroom and the W.C. is separate, so you will only have the job of asking again, so try asking for "the loo". This is a word in common use nowdays. It was mainly used by theatrical people and the like at one time, but since TV has invaded our homes most people use the term. I used to have an interesting story of how the word came to mean W.C., but a year or two ago I was corrected by quite a famous author who had spent part of his youth in the States.

He assured me, although Americans do not know the word loo, it was, in fact, a word used by the In-set in the Twenties. They would call it the "loo-loo". I am carefully using the word W.C. here, as I discovered during my two years in an architect's office that lavatory, as I used to call it, was, in fact, a small wash-hand basin in the loo, and the loo, in actual fact, is a W.C. generally pedestal type—anyway these days I call it "the smiling room"—for if you notice; people always come out 'smiling'!

The confusion of a clothes cupboard, or wardrobe, being called a closet by the Americans to the amusement of English people, who, in days gone by, particularly in the North of England called a loo a closet. The first loos were part of the dressing room and called garderobe, which, we all know, is French for wardrobe, and also called closet. So, eventually, we got water-closet—W.C.—and somehow the Americans got to saying clothes closet, and us, wardrobe.

"Just hang it in the closet, kid."

Anyway, back to your journey by car, or should I say, automobile.

If you come to a sign, saying, DIVERSION, read this as detour. The fun I have had with these two words!

When I first started in the travel business I used to do tours I called Twenty-one countries in Twenty-one days. It was only ten countries in Twenty-one days, but it felt like Twenty-one, and it really was a case of, "If it's Venice it must be Wednesday." Well, one tour I took for an American company still sends a shiver down my spine when I think about it. These people had never been out of the States before, and the representative of the Company had not told them any lies; he had spoken the truth, carefully using European terms for things he knew meant something quite different to the Americans. As he was American born himself, he knew well what he was doing. They were told they would have a de luxe coach. Well, that is what they had. But a de luxe coach to an American means air-conditioned, but in Europe it has to state de luxe coach air-conditioned, or it will only be air-cooled. There is a difference in the price. Well, at ninety-degrees Fahrenheit, outside the coach in Rome, you can imagine the heat inside. The poor things nearly cooked, in fact it was at this point, that one lady who had decided she would speak for the whole group—stood up and announced "I am speaking for everyone here—and we are revolting..." She got no further than that, because the whole crowd burst into laughter and one said— "I bet Tracey would drink to that". So off we went—very hot— but cheerful.

The two-hundred-mile journeys we had some days they imagined would be along freeways. They had not accounted for country roads and mountain passes. They were also told the hotels they would stay in all had rooms with baths. They did. But my group were not getting them. He had said all hotels had rooms with bath not hotels had rooms all with bath. See the difference? I was left to sort out the mess and pacify the passengers.

Well, on this tour we kept getting diverted, so when we came to a sign saying DIVERSION, the passengers asked what it meant. I said, "It means we are diverted, because of road repairs or something." "Oh, you mean a detour," they said. "No, I mean a diversion," was my reply. Then the explanations came:

"No, Tracey, a diversion is something to divert your attention, to take your mind off something that bothers you. A detour is when the road is being repaired."

"Yes," I told them, "this is a diversion to us, too, but it also means you are diverted to another road because the one you should take is blocked. A detour means you have a choice of roads—a direct one, say, a shorter one but not very interesting, or, take a detour where the road may be longer but the view better." Anyway, we got diversion and detour sorted out.

Finally, we arrived at our hotel, and we have two rooms only with bath and forty-eight people, so I used my rota system, giving the rooms with bath to different people at each hotel. I just gave my usual brief apology and escaped, as I knew they would be furious. I had gone through this about seven times before and neither myself nor the hotel could do anything about it as this is what had been booked. Even if my people were willing to pay extra on the spot, which only four were, there were no rooms available. So at dinner-time they would all go down to eat at the same time and I knew the pattern: I would walk into the restaurant and they would be sat there with faces like thunder, knife and fork in hand, as if they would have liked to have carved me up, not their dinner, and no amount of light-hearted chatter made up for them having no bathroom. And this night, in Innsbruck, I thought to myself "Not another evening spent trying to eat my dinner amidst moans and groans." Then suddenly, I remembered my wig.

My friend and I had bought ourselves blonde wigs.

Anyone less likely to wear a blonde wig than me you have never seen. I look like a man in drag—female impersonator, to you. "The wig," I thought. "Put on the wig." I did. And, all dressed up and a wig that had sat at the bottom of my suitcase for two weeks brought out for an airing, now covered my very dark hair. As I went into the dining-room, they were like an army ready to attack. So I made the most flamboyant entrance of my career, and announced, in a very loud voice, "This is what is known as a diversion." And the whole crowd burst into laughter. We had a very jolly evening.

"This is a Diversion."

We have got a long way from your car journey, haven't we? Anyway, more words for you.

If you have to stop to phone your friend en route, look for a phone box. I believe, some part of the States say phone booth, others kiosk.

If you have no money and you want to call 'collect', you will have to ask the operator if you can reverse the charge. For a person to person call, we say "a personal call"; for information, we ask for "Directory Inquiries."

Oh yes. The sidewalk, we call pavement. I cannot think what that has got to do with anything, except you have to go onto the pavement to get to the phone-box. If it is dark, and someone says they will shine their torch to show you the phone-box, they are not an Olympic flame carrier. It is just what you know as a flashlight—word which some older people still use here—we call a torch.

If someone directs you to your friend's house they will not use the term "so many blocks", but will say "so many turnings"—in other words, instead of saying "You go down here two blocks, and take a right, and it is the third block on your left . . ." we would say, "Go down here and take the second turning to the left." I have a feeling you do not go around corners. Cannot remember what you say for this, but it is a bit illogical, when you think of it, isn't it? How can a corner be round? We also have squares—garden squares for instance, that are round too! So what is in a name? You may well ask.

By the way—you are on holiday, not taking a vacation.

If anyone asks, "Are you here for a fortnight?" it is our way of saying two weeks.

Oh yes. What you call an overnight bag, we call a weekend case. An overnight bag or hold-all, to us would be like your carry-on or flight-bag. The problems I have had when I have asked people to pack an over night bag: they would turn up with what we call a weekend case.

When I suggest a flask was a useful item to travel with if they wanted a warm drink in the night they got the idea I thought they were secret drinkers until I realised a flask meant the brandy type. It does to us, but we call it a hip flask. The one I meant was a thermos bottle, which we know as a Thermos flask which is often shortened to thermos.

Strange how in both our countries things become known by their trade names—for instance, here, most people call a vacuum-cleaner a Hoover, Hoover being the name of the manufacturer. Like our paper hankies or tissues, you call Kleenex.

When you finally arrive at your friends home the first thing to happen will be the kettle will go on and they will make you a cup of tea. Do not say "Before I do anything, I must wash up." Translated, this would be "before I do anything, I must do the dishes". If you want to wash-up, you say, "I want to wash my hands."

..."may I wash up?"

And reference to the faucet by your friends they will use the word "tap".

The tub, we call a bath.

Wash-cloth, we call face-cloth.

Back to your tea. The milk will be in a jug, not a pitcher. When we say "with or without" we are not just referring to sugar; it can also mean with or without milk, although so many Americans seem to always refer to milk as cream. Some prefer the powdered sort, anyway, because of the calories, or cholestrol, there are those who want real milk. If you do, ask for ordinary milk. That is what you would call regular. If you are told, "Sorry, it is finished … it is all gone", we mean we are all out.

While we are having tea, let's sort out the Anglo-American biscuit problem. Right! Cookies are biscuits to us. We never use the word 'cookie' unless it is to describe one special type of biscuit—say Dad's Cookies, or Maryland Cookies, but we would still go into the shop (store) and ask for a packet of biscuits, and then asked what kind we would like, we would say, "Dad's Cookies." Biscuits to you, are scones to us. Crackers we call cheese biscuits, although we do have cream crackers. Do not be misled by the cream bit; they are not sweet crackers.

In fact in the supermarkets we are acquiring quite a lot of American names to products. While you talk about doing the marketing—we say the shopping.

You may be asked if you would like a piece of Swiss roll, or some of us call it jam roll. This is your jelly roll. If it has a sprinkling of confectioners sugar on top, we will refer to it as icing sugar.

Food we have all kinds of different meanings to words. Porridge is your cream or wheat, oatmeal or mush, although I have heard a few Americans saying "porridge," lately. Then there is your jello. The word means nothing to us, because we call it jelly. When you talk of jelly, we talk of jam, and I know some of you have marmalade which seems to consist of different types of fruit, but if you ask for marmalade here you will be given orange marmalade. We do have special varieties but not every store keeps them—lemon, lime, or grapefruit. It has to be a citrus fruit, because the peel is the essential part of the preserve. Of course, there is ginger marmalade; this is the only one I know of that is not what we really call marmalade, which reminds me of two true stories.

Number one. Breakfast conversation between an American lady and a waitress.

Lady: "Could I have some jelly?"

Waitress: "We do not have jelly, madam."

Lady: "But you must have jelly. Every hotel has jelly for breakfast."

Waitress: "Madam, we have jelly for lunch, sometimes, and perhaps for dinner, but not for breakfast."

Lady: "But you gave some to that table over there."

Waitress: "That's not jelly, madam, that's jam."

Lady: "That's what I mean."

Waitress: "Then why didn't you say that in the first place?"

My second story was caused with my great interest in collecting recipe books from different countries. In an American one there was a recipe for peach jelly. Well, I knew this was really jam, and I proceeded to make same. All was well until the last part of the recipe. It said: "When cool cover top of jelly with paraffin." After experimenting with food from all over the world I have learnt not to be surprised at some of the ingredients and the methods. But paraffin on jam! It did not make sense. I rang my girl friend to ask her, and she was as baffled as me. We said, "But paraffin smells so awful." One has even to be careful to keep it away from food, as the smell is picked up so easily. I wondered if by some magic action the paraffin did not affect peaches, but my good sense told me not to try. I just decided either it was a printing error or the Americans had got stranger tastes than I thought. I had long ago settled for the meat and sweet and sour things, but this I could not go along with. Finally, I decided to put my usual piece of wax paper on top. It was some years later when I was discussing cooking with a group of Americans and I told my tale, and I asked them, was it, a printer's error?" "Oh no," came the reply, "we always put paraffin on jelly." So I said, "How come it does not make the jelly taste awful?" "Because it has no smell," they told me. "No smell!" said I, in a very shocked voice. "No smell!" You can smell paraffin all over the house as if you have just filled the stove." "What stove?" came the question. "The oil stove," I said. "What would you put paraffin in a stove for?" they asked. "What else would you put in?" I said. "Kerosene," they all replied. Then the mystery was over. The language barrier again. To us, kerosene (a word we do not use) would be paraffin. Paraffin we call candlewax. So you see, what I read in other words meant to an English reader "Cover top of jello with kerosene". So that proves you cannot believe everything you read.

Your candy seems to cover a variety of what we call sweets, chocolates, toffee, gums, etc., etc. Candy to us means cough candy or candy sticks, a soft, crunchy type of sweet. The former having a kind of herbal base, the latter a sugary taste to appeal to children, or kids, as you say. Hard candy we call boiled sweets. Then there is rock, a sort of candy sold at the seaside or popular resorts and the name of the place is printed right through the stick. Reminds me of my youth and Blackpool—that lovely smell of boiling sugar and the flavorings, watching them roll it out and cut it up. It was a world all of it's own. But of course, rock to you means exactly what it says, but to us we call a rock a stone. Apart from the seaside candy the only other rocks are the things that line the shore or stick out at sea.

Other eatable differences. Chips we call potato crisps, or, for short, crisps. Chips are what you call French fries. French fries to us have to be almost as thin as matchsticks, and anyway, not everyone would know what you were talking about. So if you fancy trying our famous fish and chips, ask for exactly that, do not mention French fries.

A can, of course, is a tin to us.

Corn starch is cornflour.

Broiled is grilled. We do not have the word broiled, and better steer clear of the word if ordering a meal, because most people will think you mean boiled. I realise grilled to you means barbecued, but we state barbecued if that is what we mean, and if you really want a nice broiled steak do ask for a grilled steak.

The pip in a piece of fruit we call a stone. Oh yes, a stone can also mean fourteen pounds in weight, so if you hear anyone say "I weigh ten stone," that is ten multiplied by fourteen pounds. Why a stone? Because the original weights used before metal ones—were in fact stones, (rocks).

If you want a straight Whisky then be sure to say you want it neat or on it's own. I know you feel you must ask for a Scotch, but you have to only ask for a Whisky, as you try to tell the Scots that anyone else could ever make Whisky and you would be in trouble. You would be in even more trouble if you referred to a person from Scotland as Scotch! He or she is a Scot and only Whisky can be Scotch. It goes like this, Whisky means Scotch— for an Irish Whiskey that is exactly what you ask for, and if you want 'your' Whisky then you ask for a Bourbon, or Rye, or Canadian Club or what ever. But to us, Whisky can only mean one thing, Scotch. You might remember to order a double, because a single will come as a terrible shock to your system, it just about covers the bottom of the glass and very little more, one needs ice to make it seem more, but it is a far cry from your size of a drink. Do not be surprised if, when you have asked for ice, you only get one piece. Sorry! I know, it is difficult to convince us that you really like a glass full of ice. If you want a martini—you must say "a martini cocktail", otherwise you will finish up with a glass of Martini vermouth, so we are back to brand name confusion.

Your Club Soda is Soda to us and it means just that; it does not cover orange, lemon, coke, etc., etc., as yours does. We call these mineral waters. In actual fact they are collectively called soft drinks in the trade, and mineral water is the Vichy type, but it does not stop us calling the lot mineral water. The cap on a bottle we call a top.

If you go and buy a bottle of liquor or spirits, as we call it, you will want an off license shop; you say a liquor store. You can buy almost all wines and spirits at a good off license. The poor alcoholics get their cheap bottle of wine from these stores and stand dejected and almost unwanted in some phone box to drink the contents of the bottle and ease their jangled nerves. We call them—unkindly, maybe—drunks. You say, lush or wino. And when things get really bad and money hard to find, they go to meths (abbreviation of methylated spirit, known to you as denatured alcohol). And when one sees them one should not criticise them or laugh or pass an unkind word. They have enough problems. Just pass by and be grateful it is not you.

Here endeth the first lesson.

The other type of alcohol, which you refer to as rubbing alcohol, you would have to ask for surgical spirit, and you would go to the chemist for this—your drug store or pharmacy.

A dry goods store we call a draper's. From here you would buy yard goods (we say material, or fabric), also spools of thread. To us it is a reel of thread or reel of cotton. The only time it is called a spool of thread is by professional dressmakers, etc., who buy the spool, which is a rolled paper tube, not the wooden reel, and there is approximately one thousand yards on these. A bit more thread than you would need to sew a button on. We also say spool for the metal circular threadholder that fits into the under part of the sewing-machine. The long bobbin type are known to us as a shuttle. I am not sure what you call them. Most people I have met just say a threadholder. But that sounds too simple for me. The same store would also sell snaps, or snappers, which are known here as press-studs or press-fasteners. They may sell sweaters, too. What passes as a sweater to you we have many names for, although we have picked up this word from you and it is in constant use, especially when it applies to men's wear. We have a cardigan, long-sleeved and buttons for approximately two-thirds down the front, named after Lord Cardigan 18/19th century, the one who lead the charge of the light brigade, no doubt in his cardigan! Then we have a pullover, generally a sleeveless V-neck-style. We have long-sleeved, crew-neck, V-neck, or polo-neck sweaters, the latter is your turtle-neck, and short-sleeved jumpers. I see now for ladies we also call them 'tops'. A jumper and a cardigan make our famous twin-set.

Items in the home which vary:

Slip-covers are loose covers; a pillow, used for extra comfort in an armchair, is a cushion; the bed type are the only ones we call pillows.

Wall-to-wall carpet. We say fitted carpet.
Clothes pins, clothes pegs.
Hope chest, bottom drawer.
Drapes are curtains.
Electric wire is a flex.
Thumb tack, drawing pin.
Tube is a valve to us.
A shade, a blind.

We would say a garden, not a yard, unless it was something very small, say, three or four square yards. In any case, we would probably make it sound far better than it really is and call it a patio.

Greenthumb, we would say a person has green fingers.

Bugs! Never say to your English host "there was a bug in the room". Bug to us means one thing and one thing only—namely a bed bug. It fills us with horror—as they are associated with filth. But a harmless insect no one minds. So for bugs be sure to call them insects, for indoors or in the garden.

If you refer to their dog as a German shepherd, they will wonder what you mean because we say, Alsation.

"I've been given the sack, dear."

The garbage is rubbish, and a rubbish bag or disposal bag would be the same as your garbage sack. In other words, we use the word bag, not sack. A sack to us is the sort that holds potatoes, or coal. We can also use the word sack, or say a person has got the sack; this means he is dismissed from his job. The men who collect the rubbish we call, affectionately, the dustbin men, or for short, the dustmen. I believe dustbin to you would be a trash can.

Should you want to get your hair fixed, ask for a set. We call it a shampoo and set and go to the hairdressers not the beauty parlor. We do have beauty salons, but they specialise in facials and the like, although some have hairdressing sections but not all. We use hair-grips or hairpins, not bobby pins. We say fringe not bang.

Sometime you are going to get around to money. So, a pound note we would call a note, for short, not a bill. This is to be replaced by a one-pound coin, or as you would say one pound piece, but we will still have five pound notes, etc. A bill to us could be one sent out at the end of the month or given one in a restaurant—you would ask for your bill, not your check.

Incidentally, instalment plan we would know as hire purchase, commonly referred to as H.P.

We keep our pound notes in a wallet, not a bill-fold. Ladies have complications with what we call a handbag. Depending upon which state you are from, of course, you would most likely say a pocket book, which to us would be a small leather-bound book a man might carry in his pocket for jotting down notes, etc., but not to hold cash. Of course, some Americans call it a purse, not a pocketbook. There again, that would indicate to us your change purse—something small which we use for coins and call a purse. So, if someone refers to your handbag, think pocketbook, because you could be carrying a hold-all as well, which I know some of you refer to as a handbag. Also, ladies, if you talk about a pin, we mean either a straight type, the type used for dressmaking or a safety-pin, the type that holds things together in an emergency. What you mean by a pin, we call a brooch. So, if you wander into a shop and ask for a pin, they will think you mean a tie pin for a man, they would not realise you meant a brooch.

Oh yes—men. A few items for them to mark off, or tick off, as we say—in other words, check off, to you.

If he hears someone refer to his sideboards they mean his sideburns. The word sideboard to us can also mean a type of dresser, an item of furniture used in a dining room, or, in some houses, in the sitting room.

If he plays pool, then while in ENGLAND he could also play snooker or billiards.

Try asking someone if they play draughts if you want a game of checkers.

Our pack of cards is your deck of cards.

If you are looking for the president of a company he would be to us—a managing director. The Chairman would be above him.

Anyone who runs for public office, stands for public office here—for instance, one stands for Parliament, or one stands for the Council or local Government.

How about a few terms of dress?

If you like to wear sneakers for casual wear and you try to buy a pair here, they will not know what you are talking about, so ask for plimsolls, gym shoes, tennis shoes, or try joggers or jogging shoes.

Suspenders, to us, are for holding up socks or ladies' nylons, not men's trousers; these we call braces, the same word used for the metal contraption for correcting children's teeth.

A derby is known to us as a bowler hat.

Cuffs, to us, is the band at the bottom of a sleeve, not the bottom of a trouser leg; we call those turn-ups.

A waistcoat you would know as a vest, but a vest to us is the item of clothing worn next to the skin by both male and female for extra warmth—sort of like your sweat shirts.

A robe to us is a dressing-gown, the only thing we call a robe in that line is a bath robe, made from towelling material.

Also, when you check your coat we put ours in the cloakroom.

So much for dress.

Another situation you could get into without warning which could prove highly embarrassing or amusing, depending upon the people concerned and their sense of humour, goes as follows.

If you arrive at a friend's house and you ask where the husband is and the reply comes back, "Oh, he's nursing the baby," do not think your friend has changed sex. No. It simply means that he is holding the baby in his arms. To nurse the baby in your arms, to cuddle him, or sway him to stop him crying, or get him to sleep. To clarify your meaning of the word we would always say feeding the baby. And to differentiate, we say bottle-feeding, or breast-feeding.

If two mums are chatting to each other about babies, they may ask, "Are you feeding him yourself?" which always means are you breast-feeding him; if she was not, the reply would be, "No, he's on the bottle." Oh ... Then again, if you say someone is on the bottle we mean he is a very big drinker, may even refer to a drunk. But it can also be used in a friendly way between one's friends, so be careful, as we English have a strange sense of humour. Anyway you will be sure to know if the lady is talking about her baby or husband when she refers to him being on the bottle, and then you can draw your own conclusions.

On the bottle.

If you hear them say the baby is sick, it does not necessary mean he is ill. We say someone is sick, particularly a baby or a child, where you say throw up. We do say vomit also, but it is more of a medical term. Most people say, "Oh dear, he's being sick."

Another problem. We put napkins on babies, not diapers. We do not have this word at all. The table sort we occasionally call, a table napkin but more commonly, we call it a serviette.

To talk about the baby's carriage, we say pram (short for perambulator)—or push chair.

To quieten a screaming child, the mother may call out, "Give him his dummy!" So pop his pacifier in his mouth.

Also, talk of heat bumps or heat lumps, we mean hives.

If you are forced to visit the doctor, you would automatically go to a G.P. (General Practitioner), what you know as a family physician. Only after seeing him and it was something he felt he would like another opinion on would you be sent to a specialist, or consultant. Our G.P.'s are very good indeed, and we have great faith in them. You would go to visit him at his surgery, not a doctor's office, and our doctors still make house calls—but we would say he makes a visit.

In a hospital we have housemen, not interns; registrar, not resident. When you hear them talking about the theatre it is what you would know as the O.R. or operating room.

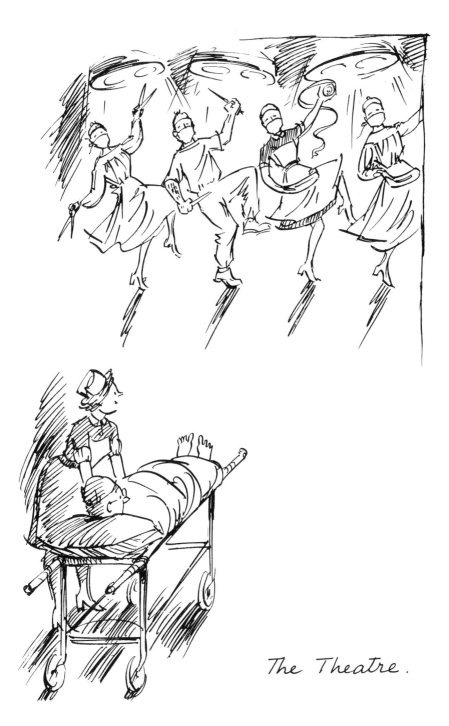

The Theatre.

Welfare can mean something different to us both, to us here it means to care for the welfare of people; in a factory or a large office, for instance, you would have a welfare officer whom you could consult on any problem worrying you. We have them in all large concerns.

Also people who work voluntarily for the welfare societies—For instance, young and middle-aged people who go and visit the sick at homes or hospital who have no one else to visit them, or just go and spend an afternoon with someone who is lonely. So our welfare workers are looked upon very kindly and they are a most welcome caller. For your meaning of the word you would have to look out for the Social Security.

Now how goes it? Have I got you confused enough? Anyway, do not get fed up if everything gets mucked up. That translates to: If everything gets fouled up, do not get uptight. Uptight we do not use; instead we say fed up, nervous, upset, offended, etc., etc. And fouled up—to make a mess of, muck something up, muddle, etc., etc. I love your fouled up and uptight. So expressive and so difficult to translate. We have so many different ways of saying what you feel when you say these words.

A rain check is something we do not use, unless you have been Americanised. We would say, "Do you mind if we call it off until another time?" Or, "Could we make it another time?" Or, "Could we make it later?"

The fall, which always sounds so romantic, don't you think? We stick to autumn. But then, autumn leaves and all that . . . and it sounds romantic, too, doesn't it?

For *Zee* we say zed, and zero, naught. Mailbox, pillarbox or postbox; Mailman is our postman, zip code, postal code; wire or cable, we say cable for overseas but say telegram for the inland one.

A wharf or pier. We say quay. We do use the word wharf but slightly different in meaning to us. Pier indicates our Brighton and Blackpool funfair and fishing-off-the-end type. They are very jolly, fun-making places are our piers.

In a movie-house, which we have already said is a cinema—Oh yes, you can always say you are going to the pictures, which means movie-house—But inside this and the theatre we call the gangway the aisle. In church we use aisle and nave in the same way you do. The intermission we call the interval, although in the very long epic movies halfway through they will flash on the screen INTERMISSION, but you will still find people saying "It's the interval."

Our schools and colleges are a bit contradictory, too, because a public school is the exact opposite of what it says. Yours really are for the public, but ours are private, and until the latter-day co-ed idea were boys-only schools. "He's very public school," you will often hear said in England. What you mean by this is very difficult to put into words. One could give clear visual examples and promptly be had up for slander. No, it really means, sort of all-scrubbed-and-clean-look, stiff upper lip and all that, and the British Empire to the last. Not that I am against all that; I am the sort of person who would prefer to see England being England and not Europe to the extent of its sinking amidst strains of 'Land of Hope and Glory', and as it gurgled away leaving nothing but the good old Union Jack above the waterline, shouting, "We were not defeated".

You also have semesters, two a year, and we have terms, three a year.

We have headmasters and headmistresses. Now, do not be naughty! It has got nothing to do with call-girls, it merely means principal, to you.

After your last saucy remark, I feel we know each other well enough to get to the other stories now, but before we start off, a few last-minute words.

Scotch Tape is sellotape to us.

Band-aid, Elastoplast.

Ace Bandage, try asking for an elastic bandage or a crepe bandage.

When we talk of a tramp, we mean a hobo or a bum. Hobo, we do not use, but bum to us is your rear end, or fanny, to you. Which reminds me of a story . . . But before we go off on that track, let's clear up tramp. Tramp just means a man of the road, of-no-fixed abode sort of thing, not a woman of the streets or the like. I guess you would translate tramp into English as tart or even prostitute. You can hear people say ". . . the old bag" this is an abbreviation of baggage. It can be used in an insulting way—but mostly humourously. In the north of England it was used, e.g.: "She's no better than she ought to be—she's a baggage that one is". So you can imagine the jokes (funnies) we can make of this.

"May I leave my baggage with you?"

Anyway, to the story.

This happened in the lobby of a very nice hotel in the West End of London. The group, having been checked in at 11 a.m. had to wait sometime for their rooms, as rooms are not vacated until noon in England. One lady got very impatient, and kept asking why she did not have her room. I tried to pacify her, and sat her somewhere comfortable and explained we had to wait for the rooms to be made up, or fixed as you would say. After another fifteen minutes she got up, and, in a loud voice, exclaimed, "If I sit here any longer, my fanny will get stuck to this chair." The whole of the English staff of the hotel in a state of shock gave a quick intake of breath and tried to busy themselves. The receptionist did not even look up; he just wrote at double speed and tried to pretend he was not there at all. After a great "Sh! madam" she got more furious, and repeated the sentence even louder. I rushed over to her, and enlightened her to what she was, in actual fact, saying, "If I sit here any longer my pussy will get stuck to this chair." With a look of horror, the poor lady beat a hasty retreat to the loo and locked herself in, refusing to show herself until I went and told her her room was ready and was not seen the rest of the day.

You see how easily a lady can lose her reputation with the language barrier?

Do be careful when shopping (marketing) for the simplest things. You have no idea the trouble it can cause. For instance, if you go to the stationers to buy an eraser, here you will be all right, they will understand, but the common word for it here is a rubber (short for India rubber). So if you go into the chemist, and ask for a rubber, do not look surprised when they send you to the stationers, because we call them durex—again, a trade name, which they have become known as, but the real name contraceptive, condoms.

When you come to a simple thing like a period, we would never dream you were talking about a full stop, we would think you were talking about a ladies monthlies—or a period of time.

Now, I thought I had run out of words, but have just learnt two more.

Way back I spoke about scheduled flight, never knowing you called them commercial flights.

And, finally, a road accident we call a crash, not a wreck.

I have just heard also where a road sign here would read GIVE WAY, yours would read YIELD. The mind boggles!

Here is the story I have saved until last, because it still gets a laugh.

One of the first tours I did with the Americans, knowing of all the things that could go wrong, at least we spoke the same language. Little did I know . . .!!!

At the end of the first day, with an early rise the following morning, some of the passengers in the coach asked "How will we wake up so early tomorrow?" "Oh, do not worry," was my reply. "You will be knocked up." Great laughter followed this, and one man asked me to repeat what I had said, and I did. Again, uncontrollable laughter. I thought they were laughing at my accent. They said, "Who will do it? You?" "No." So pulling myself up to all of my five feet two and a half inches I said, with dignity—"No, the chambermaid or the porter will come and knock you up." They had me repeating it about three times, and I thought, "What is the matter with these people—are they deaf, or what?" The following two days we went through the same story, until finally one man came up and told me what I was saying. For the benefit of our English readers, I was telling them they would get a bunk up in the morning, ("to knock someone up"— means "to make pregnant") so you can imagine their surprise when I told them there was professional knockers-up. They said that was the job they had been looking for all their lives. You see, in the north of England, when people had to be up very early for work in the factory or coal mines, some had to be up at four in the morning, and there was no being late in those days, as jobs were hard to find. Alarm clocks were a luxury very few people could afford, so the professional knocker-up came into being. The job was usually done by a man who had been disabled in a factory or a mine and was no longer employed. You would tell him what time you wanted to be awakened and which days and also very important you showed him the window of the bedroom you would be sleeping in. He carried a very long pole with a great cluster of twisted wire on the end of it and would knock or rattle on the window you had indicated until you opened the window and let him see you were awake. And believe me, there was no chance of sleeping through it.

The Knocker-up.

I remember when I was in the theatre at Oldham and I stayed with a family in a pub, called the Boltmakers Rest. The first morning of my stay I was awakened by what sounded like something from a science-fiction film trying to get in the window, I was horrified to see a strange creature trying to get in at me. It only stopped its attempt to get in when a window in the next room was opened and a voice called, "Alright, Fred!" They explained to me later that they had given me their bedroom and forgotten to leave a note for the knocker-up. This of course, goes back some thirty years, and the knocker-up was dying out then. But I assure you, not a hope of sleeping over whatever time you had to be up. The charge was about tuppence a week (two old pennies to you).

I have told this story so many times to the amusement of all Americans who have heard it. I must say, you probably never hear it said nowdays unless you go out of the city, as in London, the hotels now know not to say it.

Oh, well, we have come a long way since our first word, haven't we?

And now, how to end?

I think the best way is to have the last word. A delightful lady, who I hope will not mind me mentioning her name—or, on second thoughts, I had better call her Miss N or was it Mrs? I never can remember—but what is sure I will always remember her. She came from Tallahassee and was a social anthropologist she really understood people and could always come up with the right answer, and so amusing and so human. One of her now 'top-that' stories went as follows.

I was talking to the passengers in the bus, and you know how we have words that are the same but a slight difference in pronunciation—for instance, tomaydo and tomarto. I can never remember the word in question when I tell this story, so let's say it was tomarto. No sooner had I said it when a lady said, "You mean tomaydo". So, on I went and the same word came up again. Once more the lady said in a very pronounced tone, "Tomaydo", I ignored it. Some minutes later again I said "Tomarto," only to be corrected again. Miss N said, "Tracey, why don't you tell her you have been saying tomarto in England a helluva lot longer than we have been saying tomaydo." Everyone laughed, including the lady in question.

And so, on that note I will end, as I do hate books that go on for pages long after the story's been told.

Afterthought

Twenty-four days and some dollars later, I returned from visiting the States—I had a fabulous time and was made so welcome—but that's another story.

Anyway a few more words for you before we part.

What you call a Savings Bank we call The Building Society. A Realator would be our Estate Agent and your Real Estate office would be our Estate Agents office. I also discovered your traffic crossings—say "Walk" and "Don't walk" which seems very reasonable to me, but we say "Go" and "Stop" or "Halt" and "Cross". Our latest ones have a little red man standing still for "stop" and a little green man in the action of walking for "go".

Some people said it was Broadwalk and some Boardwalk (seems it depends on what part of the States you are from) anyway it translates to promenade, or pavement.

The door-man at the block of flats—sorry the apartment building I stayed in I discovered is called a superintendent not a door-man.

I kept asking where I could find a porter and I might as well have been asking in Chinese for all the good it did me—until someone came along that understood the language and told me what I was looking for was a Red Cap—saved again!!!

In England a shop or store can be busy, even a person can be busy at work and a street can be busy with traffic—but a phone is not busy, the line is engaged! Also if someone is un-listed, here we call it ex-directory.

I heard some people say the milk was spoiled, where we would say it was sour—the same goes for cream, apart from the special cultured sour cream. But then again some of my friends say that we say sour also—so you can't win can you???

Your panti-hose we would call tights and we get a ladder in them not a run.

When you say someone is mad—we would mean not quite right in the head—Quite often used as a joke among friends—saying "Oh he's quite mad"—but really meaning he is outrageous or just very funny or jokie as you say—but it is done not in an unkind way at all. No, where you use mad we would use angry—annoyed—furious—or merely—put out we say sometimes.

When speaking of a woman being 'homely'—it is a compliment. It means she is what you refer to as 'homey'. The sort of woman who lets the children keep rabbits in the back garden (yard to you) and who can make the home cozy and welcoming. But I realize homely to you means very plain or even ugly. We would say 'Plain Jane'. It can only refer to a woman you see—never to a man as I understand it can in the States.

'Chinzie' again causes great mis-understandings. To us we visualize deep soft armchairs and settee (your Chesterfield) with loose covers of a cotton fabric printed in different colours which we call chintz. Lots of brass around the place and maybe even a log fire burning. So remember 'Chintzie' certainly does not mean—as your word does—cheap and in bad taste.

Oh, yes I discovered when I casually asked someone "do you have a fag"? I could have been enquiring did they have a homosexual son—but of course I wasn't it is just slang way of asking for a cigarette. So be careful and don't get offended if someone says "like a fag dear"? Another is, if someone is downhearted or sad and one wants to cheer them up or encourage them to cheer up one says cheerfully to them "Keep your pecker up"—which really is another way of saying "keep your chin up"—which we use as well.

So on that cheery note, with your pecker kept up—I will leave you all.

See you around—Maybe on one of my tours?

NOTES

ENGLISH
FOR
AMERICANS

WITH A SENSE OF HUMOUR

* * *

PLEASE SEND ME _____ COPIES OF YOUR

BOOK AT $5.50 PER COPY INCLUDING AIRMAIL POSTAGE.

FOR BULK ORDERS PLEASE ENQUIRE AT ADDRESS BELOW.

Name _____

Street _____

City _____ State _____ Zip Code _____

PLEASE MAKE CHEQUES PAYABLE TO:

M. TRACEY
40 ST. JAMES'S GARDENS, LONDON W11 4RF

PRICE SUBJECT TO CHANGE WITHOUT NOTICE

NOTES

NOTES

NOTES

NOTES